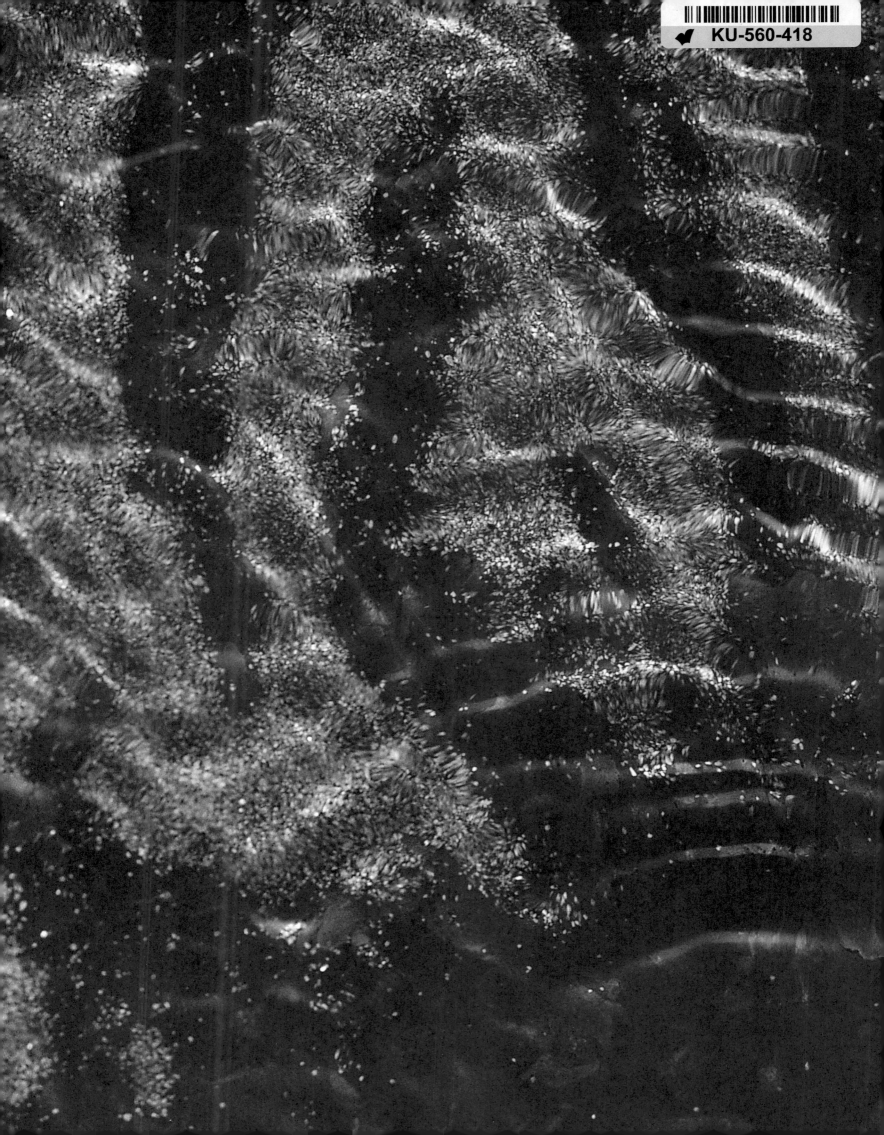

ORKNEY
Pictures & Poems

IN MEMORY
OF
GEORGE MACKAY BROWN

you have inspired
and touched us all
Thank you.

ST. MAGNUS DAY 1996

To Fay

Gunnie Moberg would like to thank
Richard Hamilton for printing the black and
white photographs for this book.

First published in Great Britain in 1996 by
Colin Baxter Photography Ltd, Grantown-on-Spey, Morayshire, Scotland

Photographs Copyright © Gunnie Moberg 1996
Poems Copyright © George Mackay Brown 1996
All rights reserved

A CIP catalogue record for this book is available from the British Library
ISBN 1 900455 07 2

Printed in Hong Kong

ORKNEY

Pictures & Poems

Gunnie Moberg
George Mackay Brown

Colin Baxter Photography Ltd, Grantown-on-Spey, Scotland

Pictures & Poems

Three

The eye of the camera seeks patterns
On shore, on hill, in fields and lochs,
        And at all seasons. The swans
        Rejoice in their ice prisons,

The sheep, sea music all round their jail,
Have inbuilt faith that dew and green croppings
        Wait their release.
        Even children among beach waves

Are incarcerated in the sweetness of bone.
(The shackles lie, under Warbeth stones.)
        And what of the seamen
        In their wooden cells

Daring, over centuries, the rocks of Orkney
And wrecked despite the web of warning
        From Rinansay to Swona
        The flaming winter beacons?

It hasn't changed much since Skarabrae
Folk plucked fleeces and ears of corn
        And set out in skin boats
        For lobsters, under Yesnaby,

And women heard anxiously a sudden wind-growl.
The patterns were there, for withering eyes
        To stook and store
        In granaries of story and legend.

A century or more since, the recording
Eye of the camera looked on the chaos
        Of history and the psalmist's
        Brief seventy years; and now

We may note, page by page, the new
And the old works of time; how all
        Fall into ruins, or go dancing
        Towards green April harps.
        Forever, somewhere, are joy and dancing.

One

Churchill Barriers

That islanders in five islands should wake one morning
And say, 'I am an islander no more!'

An enchantment is gone from his days.
Think of Prospero's island,
Tir-Nan-Og, Tahiti, the great Blasket.
In an island, time is a simple pure circle.

And now islanders would trade the sea-girding word
For the number, the new magic.

Technology gave the sea-wolf
That sank its jaws four times in the *Royal Oak*.
Engineers
Locked the four gates against the ebb and flow.

Italian prisoners, Glasgow navvies
Laboured to throw this road across five islands.

What does Time say, in its circuits?
'Spider-web, Earl's Palace, sea stack –
I bring all to ruin
And to new beginnings.'

Will the stars shine over islands again?
Will sails fly from shore to shore to shore?

Martello Tower

They bruised a shoulder of Hoy,
Opened a quarry to the sun,
Scattered a thousand squared stones.

Builders and engineers
Wove us into this thick round tower
Two centuries since
To keep the herded convoys safe
From Yankee privateers.

Twin Martello towers – Crockness,
Hackness –
We stood there like saga heroes
– Cubbie Roo, Sweyn Asleifson –
To hurl fire and iron against ill-comers
To Longhope Bay.

But the enemy
Never fell on the havened cargoes.

Here I stand still, one useless giant,
A Samson blinded.
Better my stones had been left in peace
        In the ancient hill.

Rusk Holm

Once in a blue moon
    When the moon drags the black waves high
    And a wild sea wind
    Treads like a loping wolf the sweet shore grasses

Then the tremulous flock
    Repair to a fort in the ocean
    Like their ancestors did
    With other animals, two by two
    Into the ark
    When Noah's flood drowned the foolish cities.

(In those days all the creatures
    Agreed well. Noah had hay in the hold
    For elephant, gazelle, bison, and ram –
    And the dove
    Ate the crumbs that fell from the baking board
    Of Noah's wife and fire-flushed daughters.

All endured patiently
    Thunder-stone, torrents in the sky, the steep
    Shifting perilous ocean stairs
    Till the dove flew back through seven rainbows.)

Our Orkney storm-gathered ewes
    (The wolf gentled by the blessing)
    Will stumble out of their stone ark
    One by one, to the salted grass.

Sheep Shelter

It comes now, the weather
A shepherd dreads.

How will his flock fare
When the snow cloud covers them?

Small sleep for the shepherd
In blizzards.
He wanders everywhere
With crook and lantern, calling.

The dead shepherds
– Forefathers under the hill –
They read weathers as true as the fishermen.

They have built stone shelters
For ewe and lamb.
Blizzard, tempest, are a part of sheep-craft
As well as green pastures, still waters.

Here a St Andrew's Cross
To gather sheep
Against sudden wolves from east and north.

A red sunset –
The shepherd can drink his ale in peace.

The Old Lighthouse, North Ronaldsay

There were towers before this one.
>There were tall round towers that told ancient skippers
>'No landfall for pirates here.
>There is corn enough
>And wine and sheep and fish-banks enough
>For the hundred islanders, no more ...'

And the islanders stayed in the broch
>Till Irish or Lewis ships
>Dwindled under the horizon.

Stone tower, still you held up the warning finger.
>'Seaman, merchant, keep well clear
>Of the shoals and rocks of this island.
>It has torn the sides
>Out of a hundred ships and squandered the cargoes.
>See the fire on top of the lighthouse.
>My words burn, that your throats
>Be not blocked with salt ...'

But the ships were larger, trade more urgent.
>The flame in the steeple
>Not always seen through haar and blizzard.
>East and west the greater wings flew
>With cargoes of iron, oil, clocks, newsprint.

The tower was gagged, the flame quenched.
>A young arrogant guardian
>Kept vigil on that shore,
>With three servants to tend the pulsing light.

North Ronaldsay Sheep

'The wild horses of the sea ...'
'Bull-bellowing in caves ...'

All images in books. True horses
Do no more than dip
A hoof in a broken wave.

Here in Rinansay
Sheep and ocean are one.
Ovine pulses beat
To ebb and flow and slack.
They graze on wave-and-ocean plants.
Their flesh tastes of sea cabbage.

Year by year the island walls
Are patched, restored,
That the ancient salt pastoral will not stop.

Knap of Howar: Papay

The oldest house in Europe.

What fisherman stood at the gable end
And licked his finger
To know, was it a good wind for cod?

What woman stood in the doorway?
A wife, a daughter, a neighbour
Speculated, now shrilly, now in secrets
About the comings and goings
Of a family at the far end of the island.

Before the age of the ox and plough
A man and a woman
Broke clods with a mattock, in spring.

They bargained, anxiously
For a boat load of peat from Westray or Eday.

Here, last winter
They wrapped long breathless clay for earth or fire.
Here, in spring,
A new cry under a lark and a rainbow.

*

A million bungalows will rot like mushrooms
And this house be rooted still.

Cubbie Roo's Castle, Wyre

Kolbein Hruga: 'In my small island
    Shaped like a spear-point
    I have built this round tower.

    There is no danger that any
    Pirate or wrecker
    Would take axe or torch to this shore.
    Kolbein will see to it
    They leave with burning beards, wrists broken.

    But my fishermen
    Set creels in peace off Eynhallow
    And my glebe-men
    Follow the year in peace from ploughtime to harvest,
    On account of my castle.

    I take account of my son Bjarni.
    He sits in the tower making verses.
    He is more interested
    In the psalmody of the Eynhallow monks
    Than in my office, keeping accounts ...'

    'Spear-point (Wyre)' says Bjarni.
    'We should change the name
    To the Island of the Harp.'

    'A later poet will sing his childhood here'
    (Says Bjarni) 'among
    The ruined stones of the castle.'

    The rage of youth a few embers in Kolbein now
    And a burning coal brought to the boy's lips.

Horse Mill

The work horses are gone from 'the island of horses'
    (They are banished
      With the language and songs of the people.)

Beams sag in mills where once
    The great stones thundered out
    The bread of the people.
    (Therefore they are diminished,
      The language and the music of the folk.)

How does the blood not surge
    When a tractor crosses the hill, ploughing?
    All is not well
    When an ancient stable where horses stood
    Becomes a holiday home.

Technical skills grow; precious
    Gifts of mind and spirit wilt.
    The tongues have forgot to celebrate.

See here a symbol: the strict
    Circle of labour and dance
    From broken earth
    To the bread and ale set on the winter table.
    Technology has no tongue for praise.

Dwarfie Stane

The hermit and one lonely star –
The hermit
And the bountiful sun – the moon masks –

The hermit and the snowflake (a drifting crystal
Castle): all created lights to lighten
The soul
The road from birth to death.

Yet the soul must dwell
In its 'darksome house of mortal clay',
The better
To understand the light of the first word,

And so an anchorite
Dwelt in this stone hollow, in Hoy

And eight times, day and night
He uttered a praising word
To be a part of the everlasting choirs.

So the stone may have been, rather than
A house for dead bones.

Traveller, halt here with your dog,
At this barren inn, on your journey
From light into light.

Maeshowe

Here the masters of stone built
The dark winter round.

Here the masons built a hive
    That the dead lords and ladies
    Might eat always honey of oblivion.

Here masons and starwatchers
    Conspired: in midwinter
    The good star, the sun, would awaken the sleepers.

Sailors lingering on a long crusade
    Between Norway and Jerusalem
    Broke in here, salt-weary men.
    (Heroes are not afraid of ghosts!)
They struck poems on the stones:
    INGIBIORG IS THE LOVELIEST OF THE GIRLS
    HERMUNDER WITH HARD AXE CARVED RUNES
    JERUSALEM FARERS BROKE IN HERE

They carved a dragon to guard their writings.

Ocean closed over some mouths, later.
Some died near a burning castle in Spain.

Eynhallow: The Monastery

Blessed among the islands: Eynhallow.
Its song
Gave meaning to the fishermen at their nets
And to those who work the earth
And to those
That seek wild eggs at the crag face.

Between candle-splashed matins
And compline
(Hesper bright above Birsay)
Those purified voices
Had pushed out a boat to row beyond Scabra
– Words necessary to the labour, only, then –
And fed the ox
And turned a quern like a small stone sun
For tomorrow's dish.

The island is silent and empty now.

The Spirit moves on the deep always.
It crosses the hills of Orkney on shining feet.
But we labourers
Have lost for a while the fish-and-barley dance.

Magnus Kirk, Egilsay

Many stones
Hewn from that quarry.

One stone a child
Has danced about
    On an April morning.

One sheltered a ewe
And two lambs
    In a blizzard.

One was taken
    To mark a sailor's grave.

This one went to the mill,
    This to the boatman's bothy,
    This to a farm wife
    To keep her butter cold.

Beautiful among the stones,
    You knit into a wall
    In Magnus Kirk in Egilsay
    Laved with candle
    And psalm and incense.

Saint Tredwell, Papay

Islanders with blurred vision;
Those
Who had never seen sun or stars;

Fishermen
Who, with long level horizon-scanning
Had trouble knotting a creel;

Girls
Who were comely enough
But that – among country mockeries –
Their eyes looked two ways;

Falconers whose hawks
Had sunk a claw in their faces;

Old men
Who now had a boy to lead them this way and that –

All came at last
To Tredwell's kirk in Papay.

Her eyes' beauty
Had driven King Nechtan mad.
To him she sent
Her two eyes skewered on a long thorn

And withdrawn to contemplation:
The inner vision.

Then, whoever had bruised or blinded eye
Walked round the shore of Tredwell loch
Seven times, sunward,

And, for the gift of sight
Left a small coin on the chapel step.

Skara Brae

Here in our village in the west
We are little regarded.

The lords of the tilth and loch
Are quarrying (we hear)
Great stones to make a stone circle.

In the last of the snow
A great one died. He lies
In that stone hollow in the east.
A winter sunset
Will touch his mouth. He carries
A cairngorm on his cold finger
        To the country of the dead.

They come here from Birsay
To take our fish for taxes. Otherwise
We are left in peace
With our small fires and pots.

Will it be a morning for fishermen?
The sun died in red fires.
Then the night swarmed with stars, like fish.

The sea gives and takes. The sea
Devoured four houses one winter.

Ask the old one to make a clay lamp.
The ripening sun
May be pleased with the small flame, at plough-time.

Two

Swans in Stenness

'Freeze all the lochs,' sang the ice that winter.
'Let small birds fall from fence-posts.
Let the sun
Be a gray blur to the sunk trout.'

'Take crystal keys,' sang the ice
At the famous waters.
'Change them to clanging lock-ups:
  Swannay, Kirbister, Boardhouse,
    Harray, Skaill, Hundland.'

The company of swans
Purer and prouder than the snow, sang silently
  Touch us here, if you can, in Stenness
  That is open always
  To the warm Atlantic Drift.

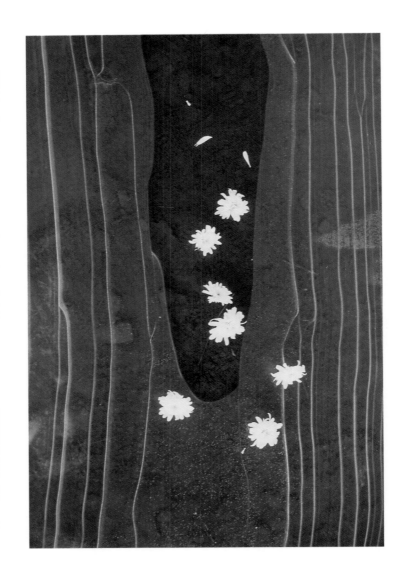

Flowers on Ice

Ask the flower:
　　　How long are you with us?
'A month and a day.'

And the ice,
　　　'I stayed last time
　　　Ten thousand years.
　　　Now I send a winter greeting or two.
　　　I'll come again, traveller.'

Pebbles in Ice

A glacier dragged us
    All the way from the north.

Did he dump us like a dustman?

No, he dropped us
    Here, from his hand, like a jeweller.

Swans

Out on the loch, white blown blossoms!

All summer long,
    A troop of princesses.

They smash the glass of the loch,
    Gently, gently.
    They seek the reeds under an ancient stone.

The blue and the gold will never end.
Summer will never end.
    But the fields about the loch
Change, slowly, from green to gold.

You are the steadfast ones.
Other birds fly north and south
Seeking the ice, questing for the sun.

But winter finds you. See,
    It hovers about you, first snowflake,
    Out of the dark cloud
    A trillion hexagons, purest crystal.
And the hill, when the cloud is broken
    Whiter than the proud birds.

Their blue and silver palace a prison,
    They walk on the ice of exile, those princesses.

Storm in Hoy Sound: Kirkyard

Such winter tempest in Hoy Sound! The Stromness dead
Have locked doors betimes against the onset.

This one a farmer –
He has left stooks and oxen
For this quiet glebe above the sea.

And this, a merchant,
He got tired of cargoes and bills of lading at last.
Silence is the best seal.

Ellen Dunn, aged sixteen.
'Stop for a moment, youthful passer-by,'
Pleads Ellen from her threshold.
    A mason has carved her song on a stone.

Ikey, tinker: 'I rest better here
Than under the lee of a dyke at snow-time
Whistling
To stop the clatter of my teeth.'

Three centuries of seamen
Came safe to haven here.
Fishermen
Have crashed through harps of water
    Into this peace.

The toilers of sea and land,
    Those Johnsmas dancers,
Are hearing, if any, a deeper reel.

The Sound today scrolled with black music.

Innumerable souls, they bide
Till the sons of the morning touch their tongues.

Hoy Sound: The Warbeth Shore

All the seven ages of man
    Wore the masks on this coast.

Children
    Built castles, dipped toes (shrilling)
In new cold
    Atlantic waters.

(Whatever the play, however
    Flesh grieved or delighted
The hills stood unchanging,
    Graemsay had its two white guardians,
      Ocean pulsed twice a day.)

Girls plucked summer seapinks, boys
    Rifled rockpools for whelks.

Above the sea-banks, the farms
    – Clook, Pow, Glebe –
Let the cows loose on new salt-tasting grass.

Legends chanted: how *Shakespeare*,
    Carmenia – trawlers – wrecked here
      And Hamnavoe lifeboatmen
    Plucked, perilously,
Fish-men from comber and rigging.

Old men's stories. Soon enough
    All that innocence,
Pastoral, tragedy, gathered
    To a good silence,
    The kirkyard on the far shore.

Thistles

Walk along the way of our year
Past the stations
Of snowdrop, crocus, the

Marvellous green trumpets opening
To announce
Voar, spring, Easter,

A troop of yellow coats, daffodils
Jostling in ditches,
Laughing along the wind;

The fluent tulips;
The poppies like blood splashes;
The rare secret

Yesnaby primula
That will not root
In sealess rockeries, southward;

Rose; sea pink; meadowsweet ...
But few praise
The tinker thistle, the outlaw:

Knives in his belt, whetted,
A tall swaggerer going
With his tribe down

Lost lanes of summer.

Bluebells at Woodwick

The bluebells
ring out no magnificat
(clothed in Mary's colour)

like the Woodwick burn
with its flute songs

like the skylark
(Our Lady's hen)
Over Egilsay at sunrise

like the chime of tuskers
in Evie peathills,
     First notes in the chorus of fire

They confer in the silence
of dew and starlight

a crystalline music
so chaste, so near the springs of time
     only a child or a saint can hear

Marigolds

All winter under the earth
    With Persephone, the stolen bride
    In the gloomy hall of Dis.

Among the dark torches of Dis
    Rose, marigold, tulip.

Listen, listen! The buried marigold
    Hears, under snow,
    A cry, first water-drop!

It is the greeting, the summons.
Time will be made new.

'Go,' says the god to the girl,
'Take your troop with you,
    Take their disturbance
    Up to the sun and the wind.
    The old corn mother wants you.
I grow tired of the thunder of roots.
All summer
    I will sit at peace in my kingdom ...'

When the sons of Ceres
    Lead out oxen and ploughs,

The marigolds
Meet in bright clusters beside the burns,
    In the marshes, the loons, the wet places.

Swimmers

The old fishermen
Did not learn to swim. 'If the great mother
        Wants our bones, yield them ...'

'Pluck a man from the sea,
        The man will live to do you a harm ...'

'She gives us such gifts –
Whale, halibut, lobster, last winter
        A wreck loaded with rum and timber ...'

'Now and then, she gathers
        A young man into her chambers ...'

*

Then the lifeboat snatched
Men from the rigging
Of the trawler *Shakespeare*, at Breckness.

*

Children on a summer afternoon
Throb in the water gently like seals
        Between Warbeth and Hoy.

Selkie

Where do you go, young seal?
My salmon is returning to its stream.

Where truly do you go, selkie?
A country lass
Has stopped at my rock in the sea.

Tell us, sea dancer
How it will be with you?

I live and die
Like a leaf on a tree.
I have as much time
As the gull on the Sound,
As the girl,
As her sweetheart who loads his gun,
As the sea pink,
As Hesper bright above Hoy.

Where, young beautiful creature?
To a tryst
On a rock with a gunner.

Eider Duck

So imperilled their hatching
    Only one chick in twenty
    Escapes the pirates, rook and crow.

This one has broken the shell,
    Been nourished, fledged
    And now is gathered

Into this tapestry, flying between
    Loch and lee shore
    Free as spindrift or thistledown.

Shags: Mother and Chick

Young one,
You are to thank the artificer of birds always

You have not swan's beauty
Nor kestrel's cruel plummet and strike

Nor lark's broken
Scattering necklace of notes
Along the red west

Nor ducks' clown procession
From barn to farmyard

Nor gulls' blizzarding
After ploughs and fishing boats.

To be a cormorant
Is to sit on a sea rock
A lean dark tide-watcher;
Of passing interest
To photographer and poet only.

Two Cows

Said Dapple to Nell,
 'I don't know what
 They intend us for,
 Milk, butter, cheese,
 A couple of hides
 For bairns' winter boots.'

Said Nell to Dapple
 'I've heard darker talk,
 Meat-hooks, sirloins, steaks,
 Sausages.'

Said Dapple to Nell,
 'All I know, this
 Beautiful summer morning
 Is, the grass is sweet
 With the dew-fall on it.'

Said Nell to Dapple,
 'Yes, think no further
 Than one bright day.
 Farm children
 Crossing the field to the school, always
 Stroke our silk flanks.'

Conversation of Cows

'What I like best is
Grass with the first dew on it ...'

'I can't wait to lie again
Under the full moon. Pure magic ...'

'My grandmother – the farm-wife says –
Gave the whitest cheese in Orkney ...'

'Which of us, I wonder, will be trucked
To the County Show in August? ...'

'I expect it'll be Rosey,
So grand in her red silk coat ...'

'I was at Dounby last summer.
I got a rosette
And my name – Belle – in *The Orcadian*: "recommended" ...'

'You can hardly see an Orkney cow, nowadays,
The farmer says,
For Simmentals and Charolais, incomers ...'

'Well, it's that Common Market ...'

'The sun's high now. Since
We stretched out
A hundred new daisies have opened their eyes ...'

'Well, lasses, this won't do.
I hope that farm boy
Has put fresh water in the trough ...'

Stooks: The Corn Battle

Call them up!
Summon a great host
  from sun, wind, earth, rain
  to guard our children

From the power of the ice king,
Winter.
  Gather them
  in the sign of the plough,

Ox, harrows, scythe, mill stone
(They are true
  With star truth
  And truth of the snow crystal.)

The host keeps a shining order
on fields of harvest
  against the Ice King,
  against hunger in the ruined cities.

Holm of Aikerness: Seaweed Gatherer

The rich web of trades in Orkney
    – Farmer, sailor, fisherman,
    Shepherd, blacksmith,
    Boat-builder, stone-mason,
    Ferryman, merchant, mechanic –
        All woven in one community.

And think of the smaller trades
    – Beachcomber, cobbler,
    Market gardener
    (The Birsay tomatoes in July;
    The green infoliated globes of lettuce;
    The new tatties,
    Pale orbs for dipping in golden butter.)

But a sea-garden! In a little islet
    A sea-gardener's hut,
    One who lately
    Laid his thousand fluent tangles in order
    For sun and wind
    To dry on a stone sea-dyke
        On the Holm of Aikerness.

Waterfront, Hamnavoe

First comers. And here
  They built bothies
  Of trees from Ireland or Norway
  And considered the true shape
  For fishing boats off Hoy and Yesnaby,
  And the two hills of Hoy
  Took note of their comings and goings.

What are generations
  But turnings of the stone pages of time?
  There were stone piers, houses, stores
  Shops, offices;
  And ships with frail wings
  Fluttering in from Bristol or Boston.
  The hills took note
  Of all ventures, furlings, bills of lading.

The stone book
  Turns heavy pages still, whereon
  The story of Hamnavoe is written.
  The hills consider
  Sagas unwritten yet, austere and beautiful.

Hoy Cliffs

A conference of old gods –
Here, a golden one,
    A rose-red crag,
    A black buttress,

A cliff with a secret cave –
Their talk more primitive
    Than the Atlantic
    Of whales, herrings,

Ships, fulmars, legends.
The names we give them –
    St Johns, Kame, Sneuk, Berry –
    Wave-whispers only.

Tide

Nor can earth, heir
of the harvesting sun
    cherish strongly
    her cold daughter, the moon.

Ocean alone
is enthralled, whatever lives
    on the trembling verges,
    shells, seabirds,

Fishermen, children, shipwrights.
Sea tilts, twice daily
    with silver surgings
    at the enchantress.

Flotta Flare

How many Flotta generations
Measured winter
        By peat-fire and crusie-lamp?

The sun
Had stored the hill with kindling,
The moon had drawn the legion fish
To dapple winter darkness.

See this tall finger of science
        Scratch the stars out!

'Let tuskers rust now, peat-folk.
Let small cuithe-seeking boats rot on the noust ...'

Be patient still, islanders.
        Do not quite forget
        Your ancient signs and symbols.

'New Fires, Old Fires ...'

We took bounty of flames to that house, thrust
Torch in thatch, till reek hid star drift.
  Then Sven, *Tell your wife, man*
  This fire will bake her loaves well,

Old blue-jowl, your shepherd, won't
Shiver tonight by a cold stone.
  The wintered ox will think
  Sun broken in on him, he won't

Stumble slow summerwards
Dragging harrows. May your bairns
  Feast them well at this flame fair ...
  We set a baulk to the door then.

A red cockerel racketed over, rats
Plopped from thatch to rain barrel.
  Burners, going back, ate snow.
  Well went their fire-song,

Its torrents drowned the small prayers,
Frantic defiance, laughter,
  Old frail peevishness.
  Dawn showed us, after

We poured buckets of snow through blackened beams
(And stopped to eat fish and cakes)
  Bones brave once, and beautiful,
  A black frail strewment.

A long time since the burners scattered
Into exile, some in Iceland, one (Finn)
  Lost in the ship *Firebird*
  Off Mey, he a boy still,

One or more to the Volga barges
And Jon gets blistering from a woman's tongue
  In Lewis, at the fish booths.
  And I this long time a sea tramp.

And Sven, fire-rouser – I saw that Sven
Or one very like him, hodden hooded
  Under an arch in Galloway
  By a candle, the mouth moving quiet.

Hoy Sound: Storm

The man in the crowsnest
    Turned his glass west.
        There, through thickening struggling airs
     Hoy, the Kame, Black Craig.
Run for shelter into Hamnavoe!

The Baltic skipper
    (Besides his chart) had sailed this way before
And measured canvas and sea-craft
    To the beating wings of the gale,
     But was glad all the same

Of a thread of flood from west,
Of a pilot beckoning off Braga.
    The salt-seeping crew
   Seemed to dance about their tasks:

In sure knowledge of ale house fires, hot grog.
    Eggs and cheese and new bread,
       Haven-fast, the black wing furled!

Swans at Brodgar

Circles everywhere.
> Everything that sets out must complete a journey.
> What appears to us voyagers a tangle, random blunderings,
Is seen, angel-vantaged, as certain as the star-wheel
Or the journey from a root that ends in the June rose.
The seed, the bequest, will quicken again under snow.

Circles compel us everywhere,
Sun and stone and bird-flight.

Ancient wisdom knew the law of circles,
> Instructing the quarrymen and masons of Brodgar
> In the purity and inevitability of stone-setting.

And the great white birds
> Caught in a random circle of repose
> Will rise soon to the blood's curve and thrust.

Three

Blockship (Parliament of Scarfies)

'Good of men, though, to give us this Parliament -
    Much statelier than a skerry ...'

'Mr Speaker, plenty of matters arising ...'

'Keep your seats. Order. One member at a time ...'

'I think we should celebrate suitably
    The antiquity of our chamber. Eighty years
    Is long in scarfie-time ...'

'It was the rage of men, no kindness
    Set down this ship in Burra Sound
    Between Graemsay and Hoy.
    Small thanks to men: their everlasting wars ...'

'Men! we do well indeed
    To keep far away from mankind, here
    On this rusted salty blockship ...'

'I wish to raise a serious issue,
    Namely, that now the *folly* of men
    Is emptying the sea of fish.
    Therefore I move
    That we quit this shore, en masse, for abundant waters ...'

'Motion denied. We cormorants were here
    Before the first people
    Straggled out of skin boats into Orkney.
    A lot leaner than us ...'

'I must voice an urgent danger, Mr Speaker:
    Oil slicks ...'

'Members must be sick and tired
    Of tourists, ferry boats, divers
    Disturbing the business of our chamber.
    Surely ...'

'The House will rise to reconvene
    When the sun touches the Black Craig.
    Honourable members will resume this debate after lunch ...'

Fishing Boats

One boat goes out in a storm
And the sea
Brims it with silver.

Another boat, another day
And the old mother
Bruises it with denial and rage.

Little wonder the fishermen
Put secret words
Into their boat talk.

There's no knowing
If that tongue controls westerlies
And unlocks the sea-chest

Or whether the ancient one
Is utterly indifferent
To all spells and supplications.

Fishermen

The purple samurai of the flood: lobster.
    The silver flashings
        On a long line of sunk hooks,
           Nets glittering like night skies.

They were in Hamnavoe, the fishermen
    Before merchants' ships
        Were built at Ness and Garson,
           Before, even, quarries gave first stones

For crofts at Cairston and Quholm.
    'Listen,' the first fishermen said
        In a sudden blind sea fog,
           'That wave has the Braga snarl

In it, pull out into flood's beginning,
    The song of Hoy Sound will take us
        To the blue and silver tongue,
           The shore women with knives and baskets.'

*

The drama goes on, only the props
    Change. Sails, oars are folded.
        New thrusts – steel and oil –
           Drive the dance to deep mid-ocean soundings.

Hamnavoe

On Monday, in hidden gardens
    The women of Hamnavoe pin their washing.

On Tuesday – it is spring in Hamnavoe –
    Small fishing boats
    Leave early for Hoy or Birsay, with stacks of creels.

On Wednesday – see – the street
    Full of country men
    With beasts to buy and sell at the mart.
    Their apple-cheeked wives set
    Half-crowns on drapers' counters.

On Thursday, shops and offices go blind.
    Men leave businesses
    For tattie-patch, rose-bush, golf course.

On Friday, in a sudden westerly
    The green arm of The Holms gathers in
    Hull and Grimsby trawlers, a rusted flock.

On Saturday, along the stone piers
    Boys let down lines for sillocks,
    Cats wait for a silver twist and flash.
    The school on the brae an empty jail.

On Sunday, the bibled elders
    Lead douce families, this way and that
    To the three kirks.

A Hamnavoe Close

The east wind
Sends its ruffians up a score of Hamnavoe closes
A week long, sometimes,
    Flashing cold knives!

And sharper than knives
Cry seabirds round the chimney-heads
When a wild westerly
Holds the fishing boats harbour-bound.

On this tranquil morning
Through a narrow defile of houses
    One frail exotic wing
Not like the rough red sails of the lost herring fleet.

Italian Chapel

No Italian had sailed round this coast
Since the ships of Julius Agricola;
And the oarsmen, that night

Dreamed perhaps of vineyards;
Cornfields; pastures
Where a sun-dark peasant

Piped to his flock beside a still stream.

But in libraries in Rome
Men unrolled scrolls of Livy and Caesar
Splotched with red of war.

Between idyll and epic
The soul of man moves forever.

We must thank the warmen
(Late enemies in a tank-strewn desert)

That here, out of rubbish and tinsel of war
On another shore
They have built this pastoral

Where all the world's peoples
May gather at an altar of peace.

Rain

When will it stop raining?
    The two boys
Have exhausted ludo, picture books, playing with the cat.

Ten thousand raindrops
Take their gray courses down the window pane,
    With gentle pulsings,
    With small music on the stones outside.

The two boys have a great desire
    To be fishing sillocks over the pier
    And getting shells at the beach
    Or kicking a clattery can on a country road;
Things only to be done
When the rain stops plucking that nagging harp.

The golden music of the sun,
    Trumpets, cymbals,
That's the music boys dance to,
    Under big bright clouds!

The sky weeps, sighs, soughs
Like an old mournful wife.

The Horses

Not wild any longer on the hills
The small shaggy horses the first Norwegians
    Saw from their longships
    (And they call an island Hrossey,

'Island of Horses', glad to see
Horses and hills in the west) after flung
    Salt hooves and manes, between
    More and Rinansay.

Farmers and horses made an ancient pact,
How the horses would draw plough and harrow
    Athwart the dark tilth
    And lead in golden harvests

At summer's end, from the transfigured hill.
Little wonder that horse and countryman
    Shared the festival at Dounby
    'The fair field full of folk':

Whisky tent, fiddles, the girls
From the glebes, the ploughmen.
    Tractors usurp the stables, but
    Who would deny the steadfast horses

Their part in the dance? Plait them,
    Mane and tail, heraldic beasts.
    Fashion them once more, blacksmith
    Bright shoes to strike flame

On the stony roads from farm to fair.
The great poet of Wyre has sung
    That the horses will return to us
    In promise and peace, when the oil-drinkers
    Are flakes of rust in the ditches.

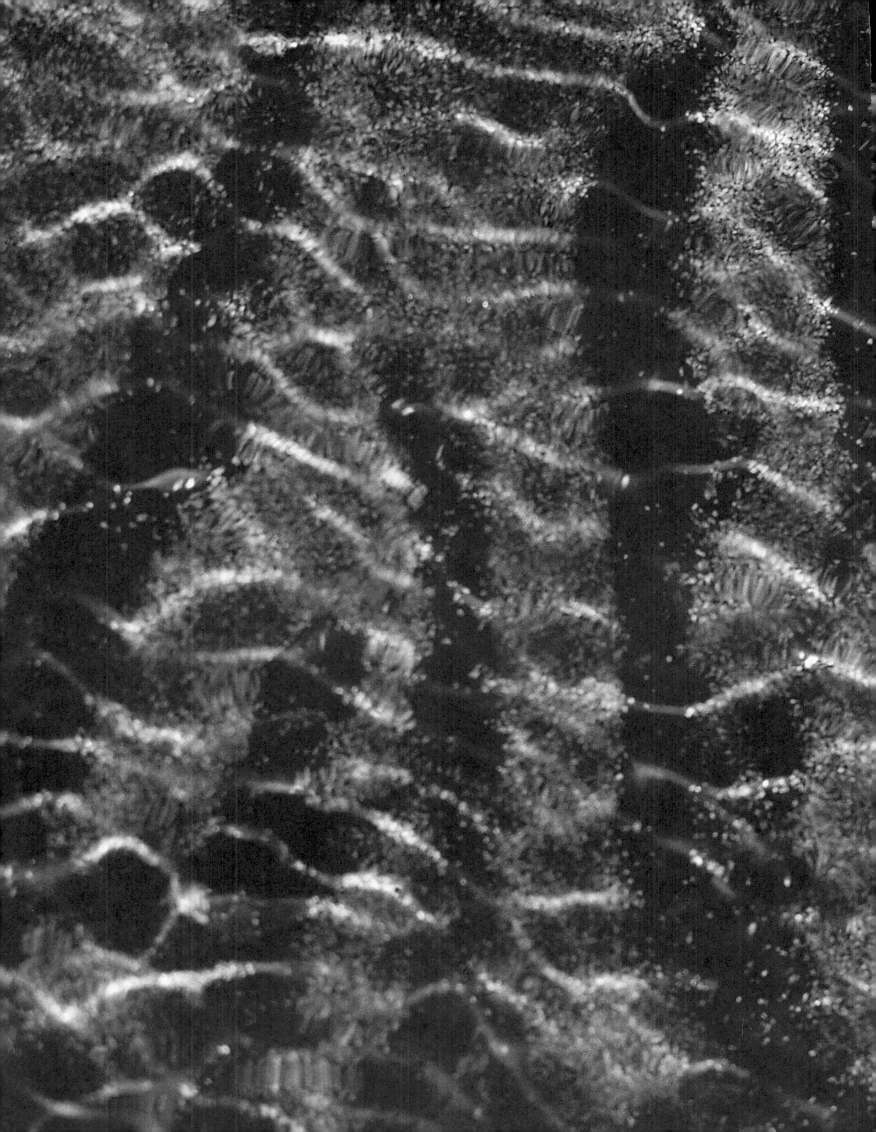